THE PHILLIP KEVEREN SERIES — EASY PIANO

FOLKSONGS
FOR EASY CLASSICAL PIANO
15 INTERNATIONAL SELECTIONS ARRANGED BY PHILLIP KEVEREN

— PIANO LEVEL —
INTERMEDIATE

ISBN 978-1-4950-6471-5

HAL•LEONARD® CORPORATION

7777 W. BLUEMOUND RD. P.O. BOX 13819 MILWAUKEE, WI 53213

In Australia Contact:
Hal Leonard Australia Pty. Ltd.
4 Lentara Court
Cheltenham, Victoria, 3192 Australia
Email: ausadmin@halleonard.com.au

Visit Hal Leonard Online at
www.halleonard.com

Visit Phillip at
www.phillipkeveren.com

THE BAMBOO FLUTE

Chinese Folksong
Arranged by Phillip Keveren

With mystery (♩ = 88)

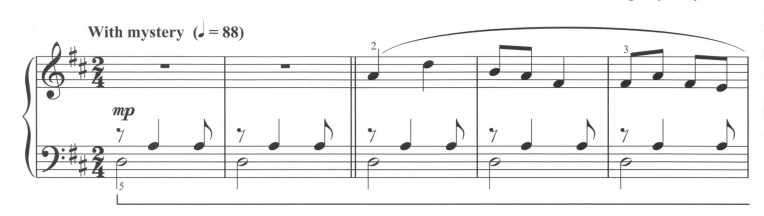

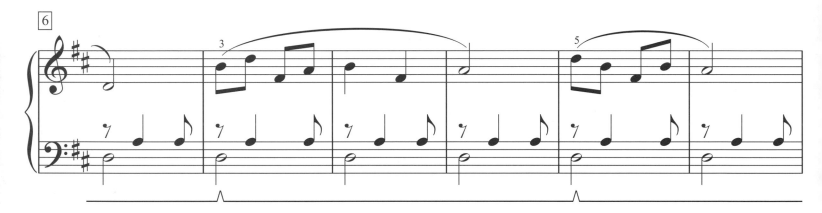

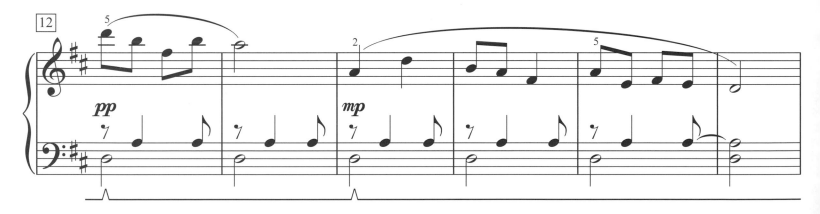

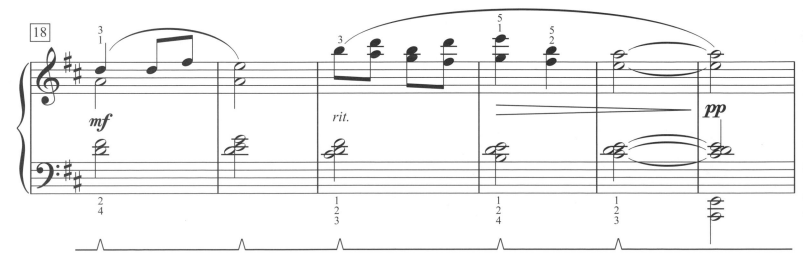

3

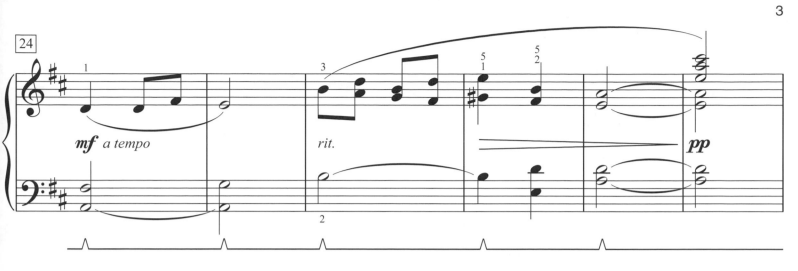

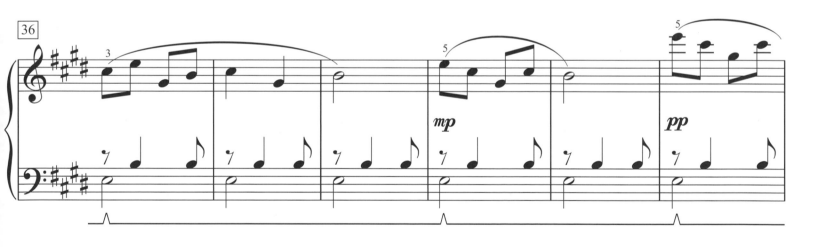

CIELITO LINDO
(My Pretty Darling)

By C. FERNANDEZ
Arranged by Phillip Keveren

Briskly (♩ = 184)

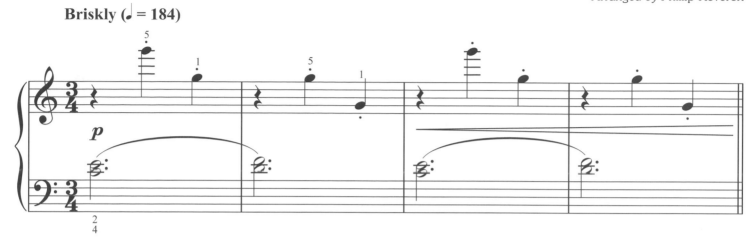

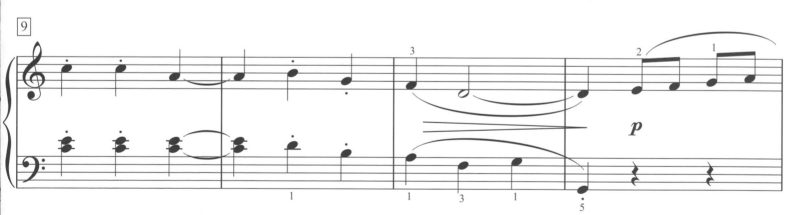

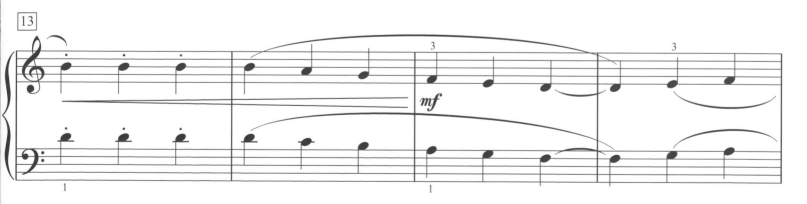

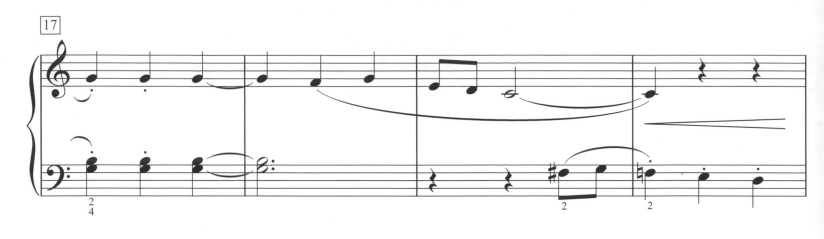

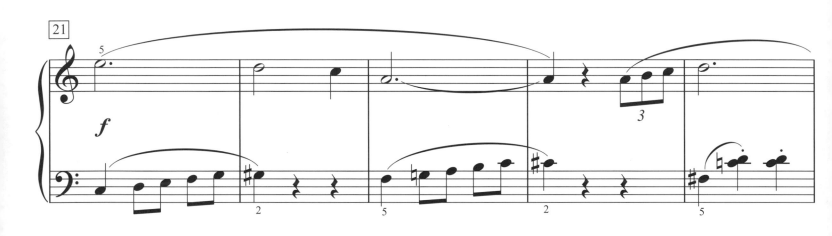

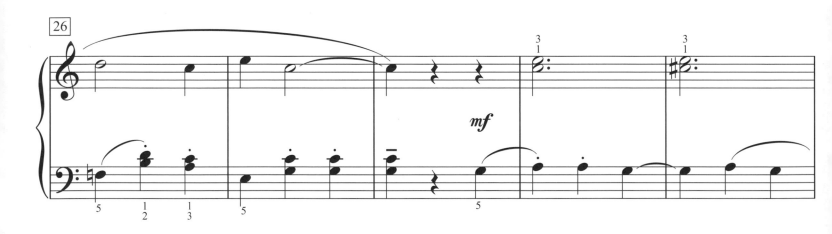

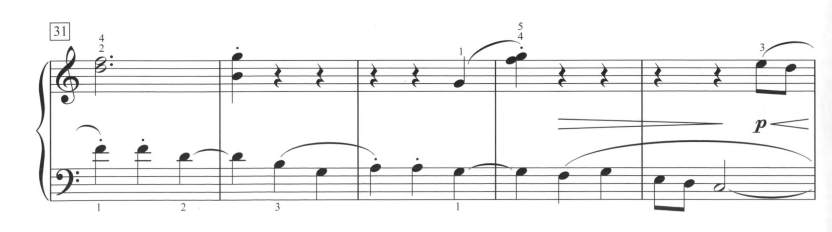

DANNY BOY
(Londonderry Air)

Words by FREDERICK EDWARD WEATHERLY
Traditional Irish Folk Melody
Arranged by Phillip Keveren

With longing (♩ = 69)

DOWN IN THE VALLEY

Traditional American Folksong
Arranged by Phillip Keveren

Moderately bright (♩ = 120)

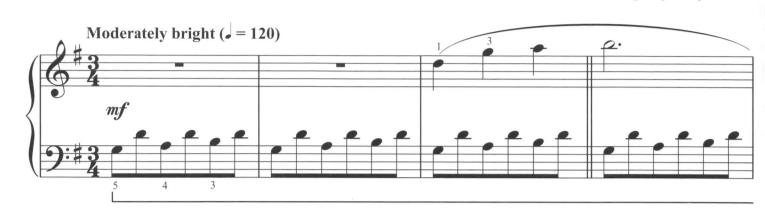

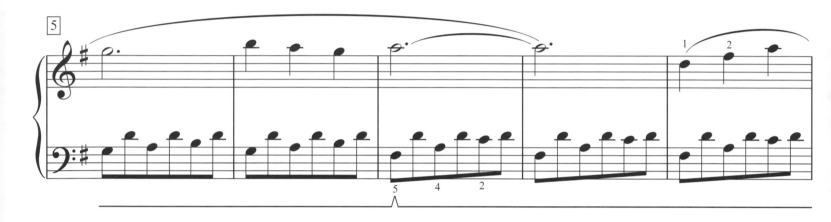

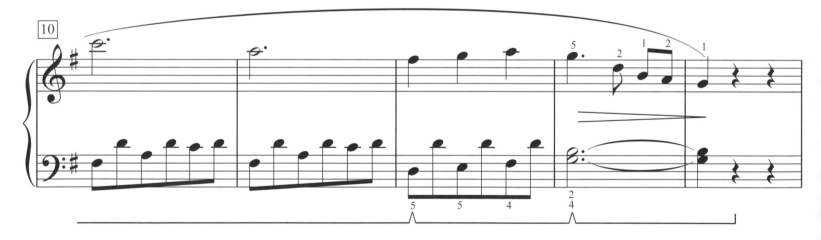

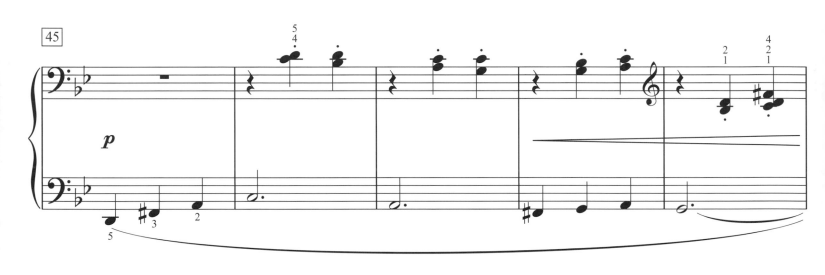

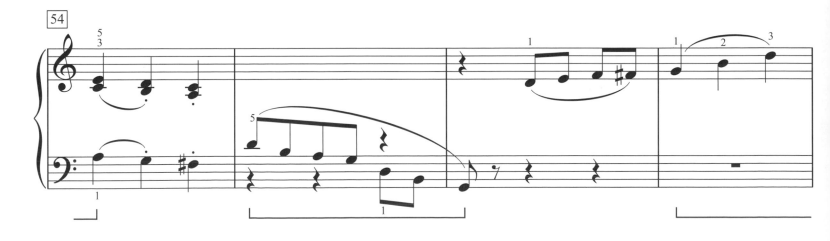

FRÈRE JACQUES
(Are You Sleeping?)

Traditional
Arranged by Phillip Keveren

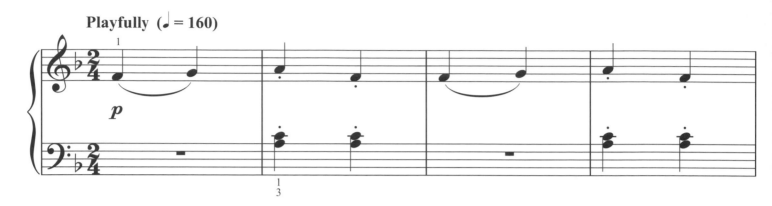

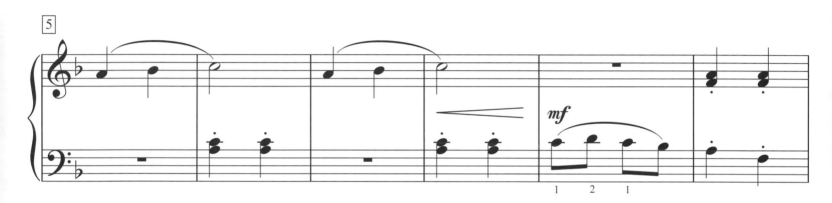

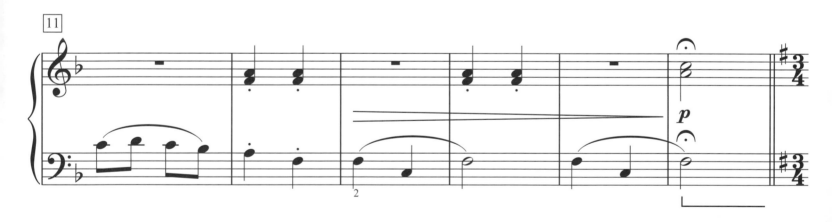

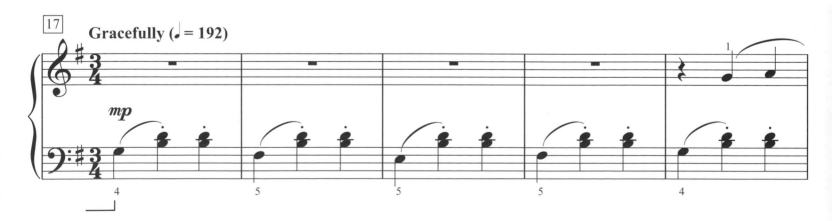

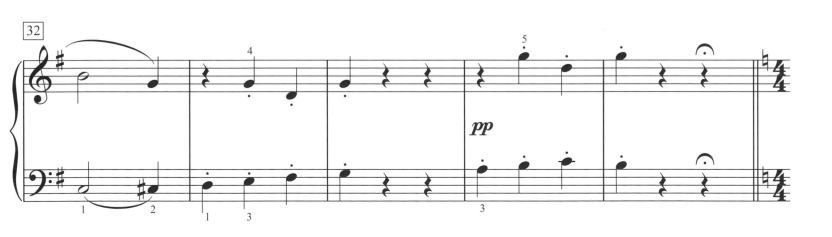

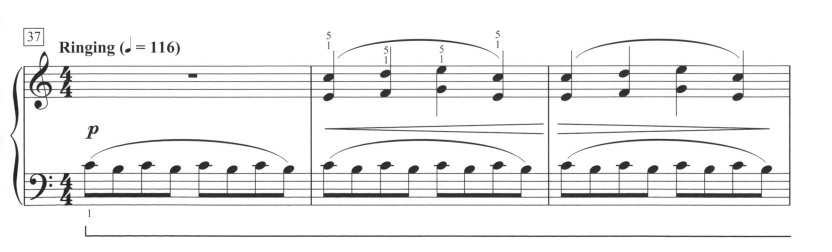

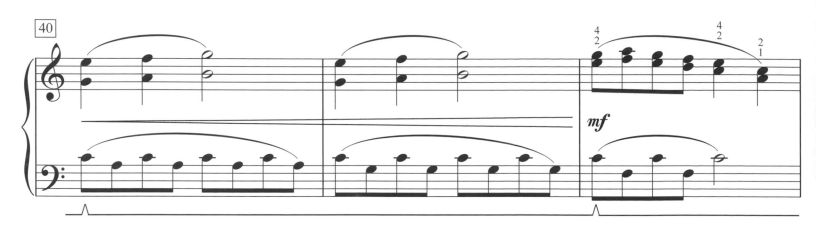

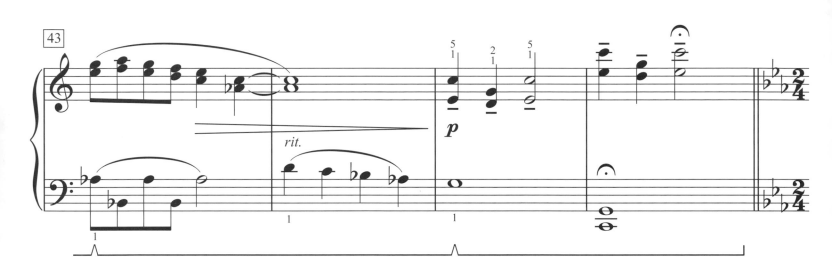

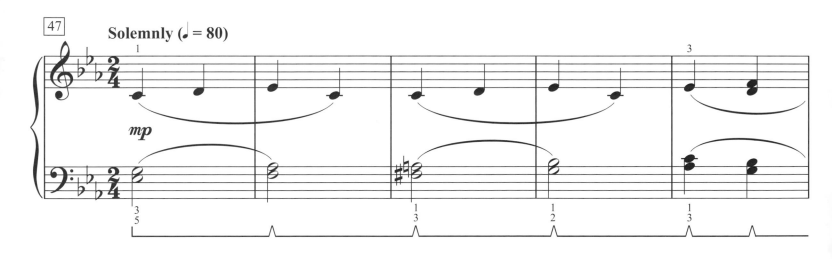

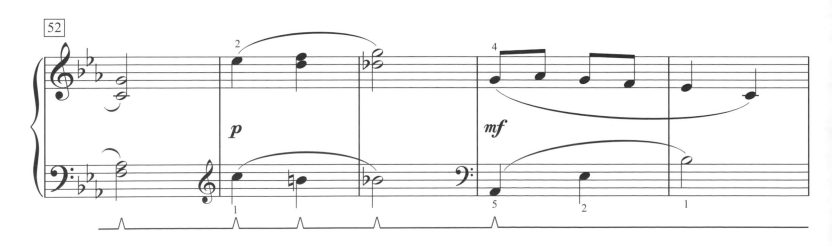

THE GALWAY PIPER

Irish Folksong
Arranged by Phillip Keveren

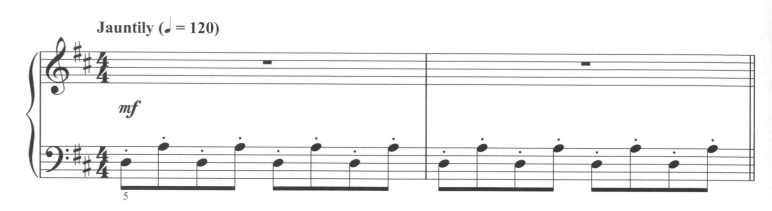

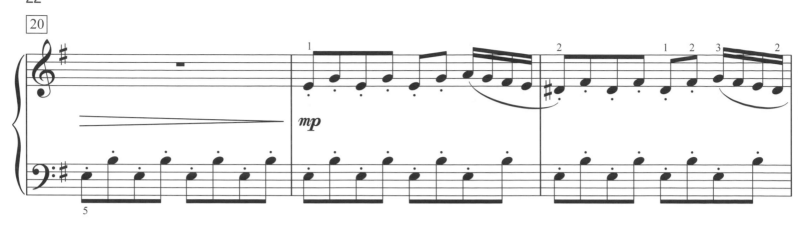

GUANTANAMERA

Cuban Folksong
Arranged by Phillip Keveren

With animation (♩ = 116)

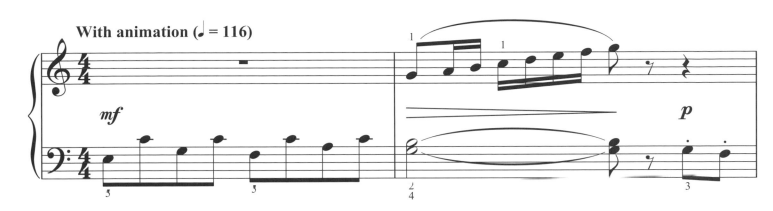

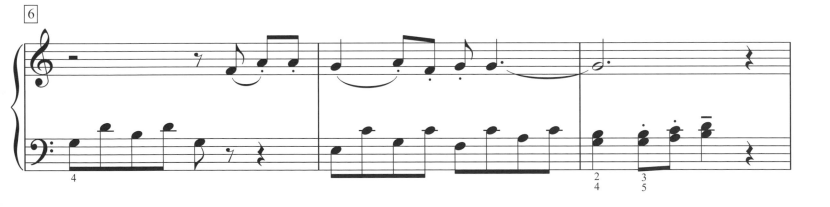

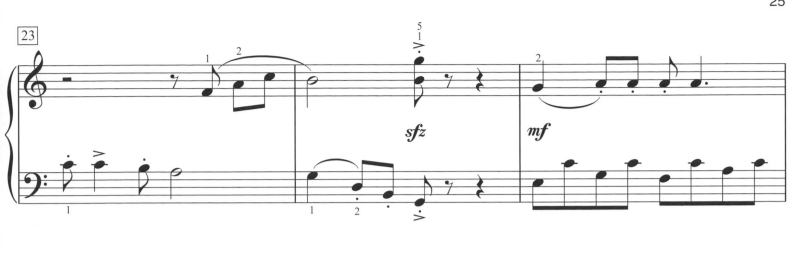

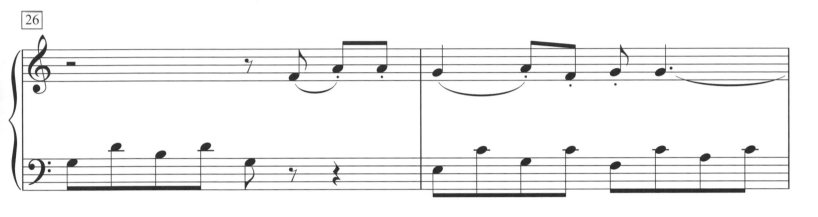

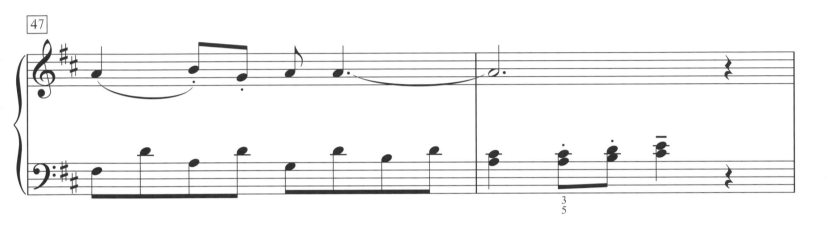

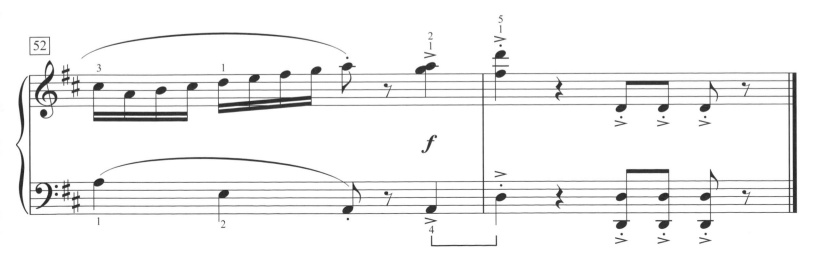

HATIKVA
(With Hope)

Traditional Hebrew Melody
Arranged by Phillip Keveren

HOME ON THE RANGE

Lyrics by DR. BREWSTER HIGLEY
Music by DAN KELLY
Arranged by Phillip Keveren

THE WATER IS WIDE
(O Waly, Waly)

Traditional
Arranged by Phillip Keveren

34

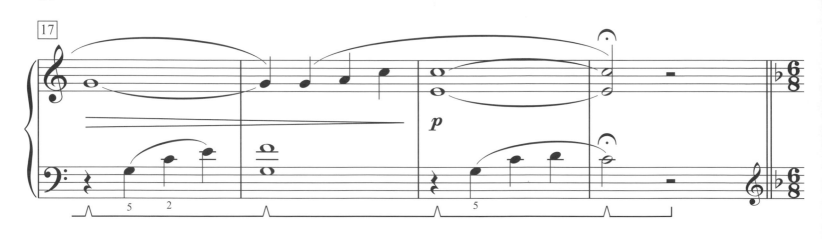

IROQUOIS LULLABY

Canadian Folksong
Arranged by Phillip Keveren

SAKURA
(Cherry Blossoms)

Traditional Japanese Folksong
Arranged by Phillip Keveren

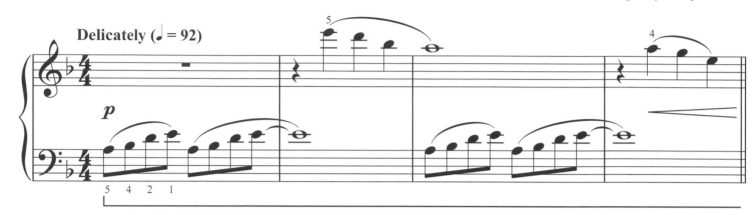

'TIS THE LAST ROSE OF SUMMER

Words by THOMAS MOORE
Music by RICHARD ALFRED MILLIKEN
Arranged by Phillip Keveren

YANKEE DOODLE

Traditional
Arranged by Phillip Keveren

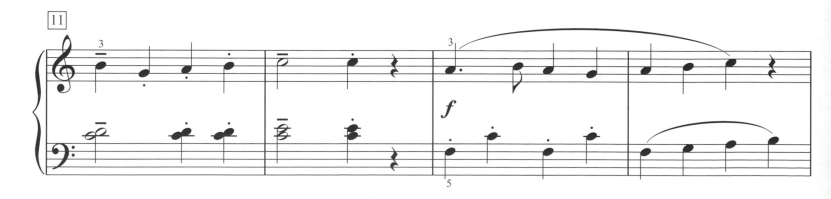

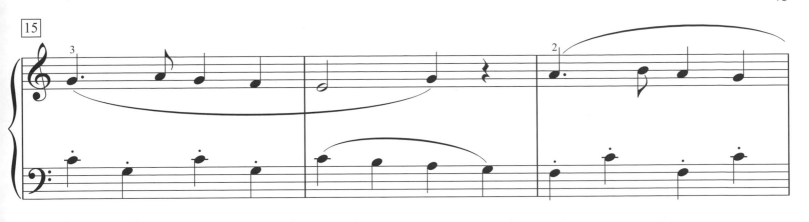

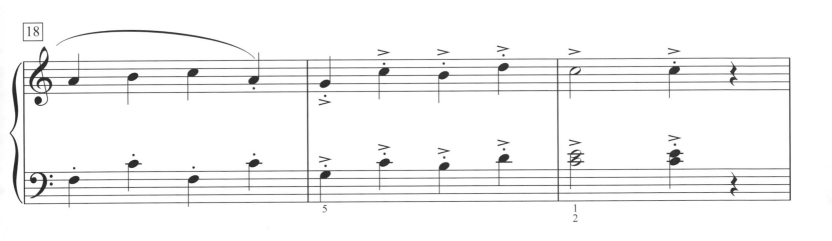

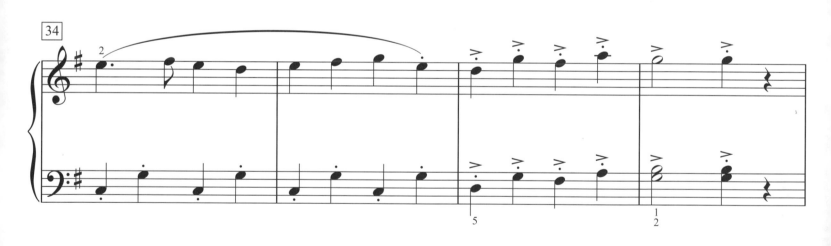

WAYFARING STRANGER

Southern American Folk Hymn
Arranged by Phillip Keveren